# VEGAN SLOW COOKER COOKBOOK

*Easy And Delicious Slow Cooker Recipes for Busy People and Healthy Eating*

*by Susan Lombardi*

**Disclaimer**

All erudition supplied in this book is specified for educational and academic purposes only. The author is not in any way in charge of any outcomes that emerge from using this book. Constructive efforts have been made to render information that is both precise and effective, but the author is not to be held answerable for the accuracy or use/misuse of this information.

**Foreword**

I would like to thank you for taking the very first step of trusting me and deciding to purchase/read this life-transforming book. Thanks for investing your time and resources in this product.

I can assure you of precise outcomes if you will diligently follow the specific blueprint I lay bare in the information handbook you are currently checking out. It has transformed lives, and I firmly believe it will equally change your own life too.

All the information I provided in this Do It Yourself piece is easy to absorb and practice.

# About the Author

Susan Lombardi

*Susan Lombardi is a cooking enthusiast who has extensively studied the most effective diets to maintain the healthiest and most balanced lifestyle possible.*

*She started writing recipes to spread the pleasure of eating in joy without giving up the most appetizing and delicious foods.*

*Her Italian origins have instilled in her a passion for food and how important it is as a means of sociability and conviviality.*

*Her motto is "Health comes with eating".*

# TABLE OF CONTENTS

# Artichoke Cream

**Preparation Time**: 10 mins

**Cooking Time**: 2 hrs

**Servings**: 8

**Ingredients:**

- canned artichokes (28 ounces)
- 10 ounces spinach
- 8 ounces cream of coconut
- 1 yellow onion, minced
- 2 cloves garlic, minced
- ¾ cup of coconut milk
- 1/3 cup vegan avocado mayonnaise
- ½ cup tofu
- a pinch of salt and black pepper
- 1 tablespoon red vinegar

**Indications:**

1. In the slow cooker, mix the artichokes with spinach, coconut cream, onion, garlic, coconut milk, tofu, avocado mayonnaise, vinegar, salt and pepper, mix well, cover and simmer for 2 hours.

2. Divide into bowls and serve as an appetizer.

**Nutrition**: 355 calories, 24 fats, 4 fibers, 19 carbohydrates, 13 proteins

# Mushroom Cream

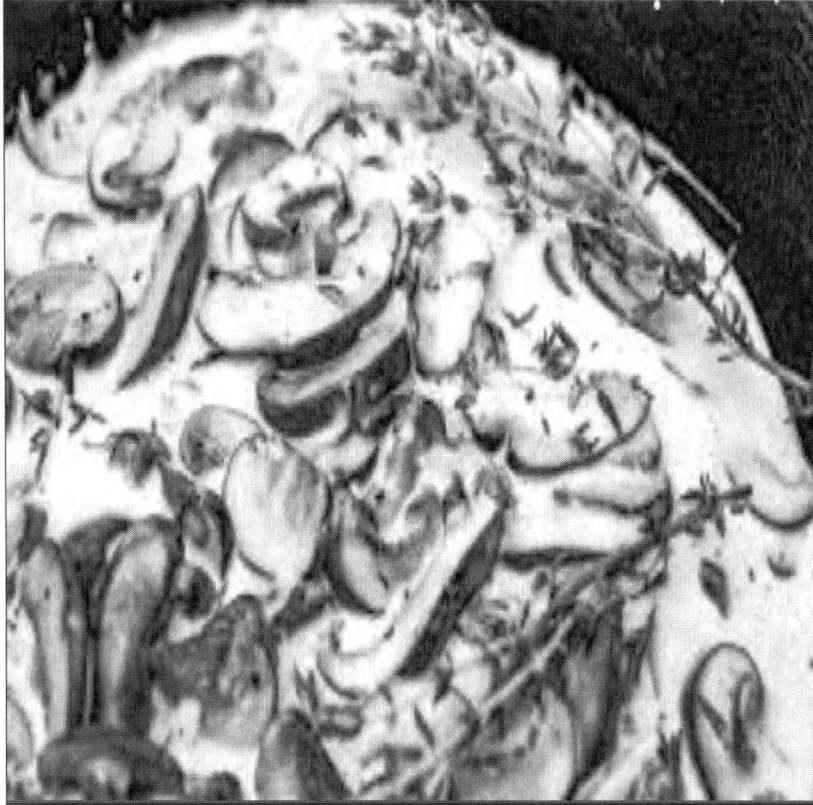

**Preparation Time**: 10 mins

**Cooking Time**: 4 hrs

**Servings**: 6

**Ingredients:**

- 2 cups green bell peppers, chopped
- 1 cup yellow onion, chopped
- 3 garlic cloves, minced
- 28 ounces tomato sauce
- 1 pound mushrooms,
- ½ cup tofu, pressed, drained and crumbled
- salt and black pepper to taste

**Indications:**

1. In the slow cooker, mix the bell peppers with the onion, garlic, mushrooms, tomato sauce, tofu, salt and pepper, mix, cover and simmer for 4 hours.

2. Divide into bowls and serve as a spread feast.

**Nutrition**: 245 calories, 4 fats, 7 fibers, 9 carbohydrates, 3 proteins

# Three Bean Sauce

**Preparation Time**: 10 mins

**Cooking Time**: 1 hr

**Servings**: 6

**Ingredients**:

- ½ cup sauce
- 2 cups canned refried beans
- 1 cup vegan nacho cheese
- 2 tablespoons chives, minced

**Indications:**

1. In slow cooker, mix refried beans with salsa, vegan nacho cheese, and scallions, toss, cover, and cook on full power for 1 hour.

2. Divide into bowls and serve as a Christmas snack.

**Nutrition**: 262 calories, 5 fats, 10 fibers, 20 carbohydrates, 3 proteins

# Classic Black Bean Chili

**Preparation Time**: 10 mins

**Cooking Time**: 3 hrs

**Servings**: 4

**Ingredients:**

- ½ cup quinoa
- 2 ½ cups vegetable broth
- 15 ounces canned black beans
- ¼ cup green bell pepper, chopped
- 14 ounces canned tomatoes
- ¼ cup red bell pepper, minced

- pinch of salt and black pepper
- 2 cloves of minced garlic
- 1 carrot, chopped
- 1 small chili, minced
- 2 teaspoons chili powder
- 1 teaspoon ground cumin
- pinch cayenne pepper
- ½ cup corn
- 1 teaspoon dried oregano

*For the vegan cream course:*
- a splash of apple cider vinegar
- 4 tablespoons of water
- ½ cup cashews, soaked overnight and drained
- 1 teaspoon lemon juice

**Indications**:

1. Put the broth in the slow cooker.

2. Add the quinoa, tomatoes, beans, red and green bell peppers, garlic, carrots, salt, pepper, corn, cumin, cayenne pepper, chili powder, chili, and oregano, stir, cover and cook on full power for 3 hours.

3. Meanwhile, put the cashews in the blender.

4. Add water, vinegar, and lime juice and mix well.

5. Divide chilli into bowls, garnish with vegan sour cream, and serve.

**Nutrition:** 300 calories, 4 fats, 4 fibers, 10 carbohydrates, 7 proteins

# Carrot Oats

**Preparation Time**: 10 mins

**Cooking Time**: 7 hrs

**Servings**: 4

**Ingredients:**

- 2 cups of coconut milk
- ½ cup steel cut oats
- 1 cup carrots, chopped
- 1 teaspoon cardamom, ground
- ½ teaspoon agave nectar
- pinch of saffron
- sight spray

**Indications**:

1. Spray slow cooker with cooking spray, add milk, oatmeal, carrots, cardamom and agave nectar, mix, cover and simmer for 7 hours.

2. Stir the oats again, divide into bowls, sprinkle with saffron and serve for breakfast.

**Nutrition**: 182 calories, 7 fats, 4 fibers, 8 carbohydrates, 3 proteins

# Delicious Vegan Revolt

**Preparation Time**: 10 mins

**Cooking Time**: 8 hrs

**Servings**: 4

## Ingredients:

- 1 pound tofu, crumbled
- 1 pound white mushrooms, sliced
- 1 cup green onions, chopped
- 1 cup of corn
- 1 tablespoon of olive oil
- a pinch of salt and black pepper
- 1 chopped zucchini
- cup coconut amino acids
- ½ cup nutritional yeast
- 3 pounds red potatoes, cut in half

## Indications:

1. In your slow cooker, mix the oil with the tofu, mushrooms, scallions, corn, salt, pepper, zucchini, amino acids, yeast and potatoes, mix, cover and cook over heat. slow for 8 hours.

2. Divide into plates and serve for breakfast.

**Nutrition:** 222 calories, 5 fats, 8 fibers, 12 carbohydrates, 4 proteins

# Oatmeal With Blueberries

**Preparation Time**: 10 mins

**Cooking Time**: 8 hrs

**Servings**: 4

**Ingredients:**

- 1 cup blueberries
- 1 cup steel cut oats
- 1 cup of coconut milk
- 2 tablespoons agave nectar
- ½ teaspoon vanilla extract
- walnut flakes to serve
- sight spray

**Indications:**

1. Spray slow cooker with cooking spray, add oats, milk, agave nectar, vanilla and blueberries, toss, cover and simmer for 8 hours.

2. Stir the oats once more, divide into bowls, sprinkle with coconut flakes and serve.


**Nutrition:** 182 calories, 6 fats, 8 fibers, 9 carbohydrates, 6 proteins

# Sweet Breakfast With Apples and Pears

**Preparation Time**: 10 mins

**Cooking Time**: 6 hrs

**Servings**: 6

## Ingredients:

- 4 apples, cored, peeled and cut into medium pieces
- 1 teaspoon lemon juice
- 4 pears, cored, peeled and cut into medium pieces
- 5 teaspoons stevia
- 1 teaspoon ground cinnamon
- 1 teaspoon vanilla extract
- ½ teaspoon ground ginger
- ½ teaspoon ground cloves
- ½ teaspoon cardamom, ground

## Indications:

1. In slow cooker, mix apples with pears, lemon juice, stevia, cinnamon, vanilla extract, ginger, cloves, and cardamom, stir, cover, and simmer for 6 hours.

2. Divide into bowls and serve for breakfast.

**Nutrition**: 201 calories, 3 fats, 7 fibers, 19 carbohydrates, 4 proteins

# Almond Butter Oatmeal

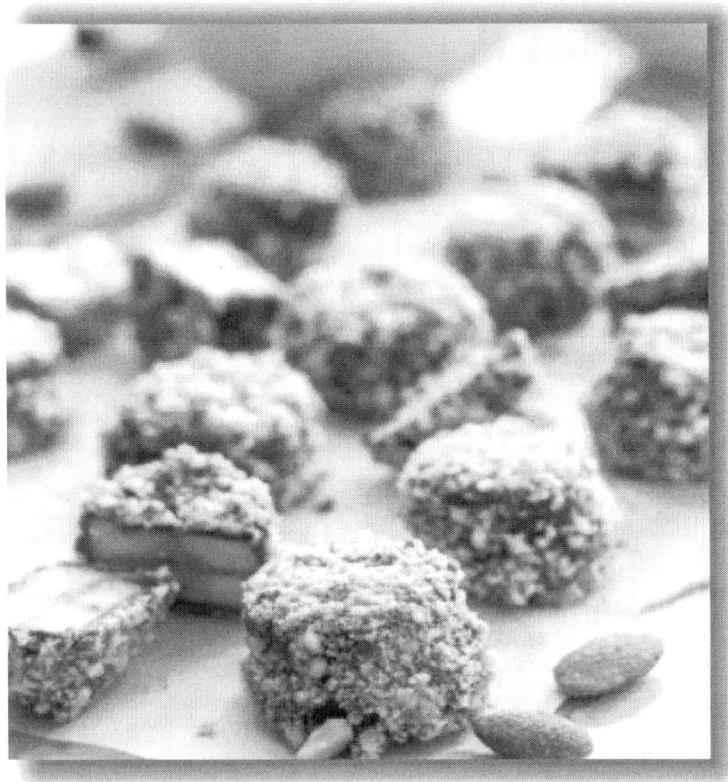

**Preparation Time:** 10 mins

**Cooking Time**: 10 hrs

**Servings**: 2

**Ingredients:**

- ½ cup steel cut oats
- ½ cup of almond milk
- the seeds of 1 vanilla bean
- 1 cup of water
- 4 tablespoons stevia almond butter to taste

**Indications:**

1. In 2 heat-resistant containers, divide the oatmeal, almond milk, vanilla beans, water, stevia, and almond butter and mix.

2. Place the containers in the slow cooker, fill the slow cooker halfway with water, cover and simmer for 10 hours.

3. Serve hot for breakfast.

**Nutrition**: 182 calories, 3 fats, 7 fibers, 18 carbohydrates, 4 proteins

# Delicious Blueberry Pudding

**Preparation Time**: 10 mins

**Cooking Time**: 3 hrs

**Servings**: 6

**Ingredients:**

- 1 cup of almond flour
- 2 tablespoons lemon juice
- 2 cups blueberries
- 2 teaspoons baking powder
- ½ teaspoon ground nutmeg
- ½ cup of almond milk
- 1 cup coconut sugar
- 1 spoon of flaxseed meal blended with 1 spoon of water
- ¼ cup coconut butter, melted
- 1 teaspoon vanilla extract
- 1 tablespoon vegan cornstarch
- 1 cup hot water
- sight spray

**Indications:**

1. Grease your slow cooker with cooking spray, add the cranberries and lemon juice, stir slightly, and spread evenly across the bottom of the pan.

2. In a bowl, mix the flour with the nutmeg, the cup of sugar and the baking powder and mix.

3. Add the vanilla, coconut butter, flaxseed meal, and milk and mix well again.

4. Pour this over the blueberries and spread.

5. In a small bowl mix the rest of the sugar with the cornstarch and hot water and mix very well.

6. Add this to the slow cooker, cover and cook over high heat for 3 hours.

7. Allow pudding to cool slightly, divide into bowls and serve.

**Nutrition:** 220 calories, 4 fats, 4 fibers, 9 carbohydrates, 6 proteins

# Tasty Pear Delight

**Preparation Time**: 10 mins

**Cooking Time**: 4 hrs

**Servings**: 12

**Ingredients:**

- 3 pears, cored, peeled and chopped
- ½ cup raisins
- 2 cups dried fruit, mixed
- ¼ cup coconut sugar
- 1 tablespoon vinegar
- 1 teaspoon lemon zest
- 1 teaspoon ground ginger
- a pinch of ground cinnamon

**Indications:**

1. Place the pears properly in the slow cooker.

2. Add the raisins, fruit, sugar, vinegar, lemon zest, ground ginger and cinnamon, mix, cover and simmer for 4 hours.

3. Divide into jars and serve whenever you want!

**Nutrition:**140 calories, 3 fats, 4 fibers, 6 carbohydrates, 6 proteins

# Easy Almond Pudding

**Preparation Time**: 10 mins

**Cooking Time**: 2 hrs 30 mins

**Servings**: 6

**Ingredients:**

- 1 tangerine, sliced
- juice of 2 tangerines
- 2 tablespoons coconut sugar
- 4 ounces coconut butter, smooth
- flaxseed meal (2 tablespoons) mixed with 1 tablespoon of water
- cup coconut sugar
- cup of almond flour
- 1 teaspoon baking powder
- cup almonds, ground
- sight spray

**Indications:**

1. Grease a baking sheet and sprinkle 2 tablespoons of sugar on the bottom.

2. Place the tangerine slices on top of the sugar and set the pan aside for now.

3. In a bowl, mix the butter with ¾ cup sugar and the flaxseed flour mixed with water and mix well.

4. Add the almonds, flour, baking powder and tangerine juice and mix again.

5. Spread over tangerine slices, place skillet in slow cooker, cover, and cook on high for 2 hours and 30 minutes.

6. Uncover, reserve a few minutes, transfer to a serving plate, slice and serve.

**Nutrition:** 200 calories, 4 fats, 2 fibers, 5 carbohydrates, 6 proteins

# Wild Wild Rice Mix

**Preparation Time**: 10 mins

**Cooking Time**: 6 hrs

**Servings:** 12

**Ingredients:**

- 40 ounces vegetable broth
- 2 1/2 cups wild rice
- 1 cup carrot, chopped
- mushrooms (4 ounces)
- 2 tablespoons of olive oil
- 2 teaspoons dried and ground marjoram
- salt and black pepper to taste
- 2/3 cup dried cherries
- 1/2 cup walnuts, toasted and chopped
- 2/3 cup green onions, chopped

**Indications:**

1. In the slow cooker, mix the broth with wild rice, carrots, mushrooms, oil, marjoram, salt, pepper, cherries, walnuts and green onions, mix, cover and simmer for 6 hours.

2. Stir the wild rice one more time, divide into plates and serve as a garnish.

**Nutrition**: 169 calories, 5 fats, 3 fibers, 28 carbohydrates, 5 proteins

# Rustic Mashed Potatoes

**Preparation Time**: 10 mins

**Cooking Time**: 4 hrs

**Servings**: 6

**Ingredients:**

- 6 garlic cloves, peeled
- 3 pounds golden potatoes, peeled and diced
- 1 bay leaf
- 1 cup of coconut milk
- 28 ounces vegetable broth
- 3 tablespoons olive oil
- salt and black pepper to taste

**Indications:**

1. In the slow cooker, mix the potatoes with the broth, bay leaf, garlic, salt and pepper, cover and cook on full power for 4 hours.

2. Drain the potatoes and garlic, return them to the slow cooker and mash them with a potato masher.

3. Add the coconut oil and milk, blend well, divide into plates and serve as a garnish.

**Nutrition**: 135 calories, 5 fats, 1 fiber, 20 carbohydrates, 3 proteins

# Glazed Carrots

**Preparation Time**: 10 mins

**Cooking Time**: 4 hrs

**Servings:** 10

**Ingredients:**

- 1 pound parsnips, cut into medium pieces
- 2 pounds carrots, cut into medium pieces
- 2 tablespoons orange zest, chopped
- 1 cup of orange juice
- ½ cup orange marmalade
- ½ cup vegetable broth
- 1 tablespoon tapioca, crushed
- a pinch of salt and black pepper
- 3 tablespoons of olive oil
- ¼ cup parsley, chopped

**Indications:**

1. In the slow cooker, mix the parsnips with the carrots.

2. In a bowl mix the orange peel with the orange juice, the broth, the orange marmalade, the tapioca, the salt and the pepper, blend and add the carrots on top.

3. Cook everything on high for 4 hours.

4. Add the parsley, mix, divide into plates and serve as a garnish.

**Nutrition:** 159 calories, 4 fats, 4 fibers, 30 carbohydrates, 2 proteins

# Mushroom and Pea Risotto

**Preparation Time**: 10 mins

**Cooking Time**: 1 hour 30 mins

**Servings**: 8

**Ingredients:**

- 1 shallot, minced
- 8 ounces of white mushrooms, sliced
- 3 tablespoons olive oil
- 1 teaspoon garlic, 1 cup minced
- ¾ white rice
- 4 cups of vegetable broth
- 1 cup of peas
- salt and black pepper to taste

**Indications:**

1. In the slow cooker, mix the oil with the shallot, mushrooms, garlic, rice, broth, peas, salt and pepper, mix, cover and cook on maximum power for 1 hour and 30 minutes.

2. Stir the risotto one more time, divide it into plates and serve as a garnish.

3. Enjoy!

**Nutrition**: 254 calories, 7 fats, 3 fibers, 27 carbohydrates, 7 proteins

# Cherry Breakfast Delight

**Preparation Time**: 10 mins

**Cooking Time**: 8 hrs 10 mins

**Servings**: 4

**Ingredients:**

- 2 cups of almond milk
- 2 cups of water
- 1 cup steel cut oats
- 2 tablespoons cocoa powder
- 1/3 cup pitted cherries
- cup maple syrup
- ½ teaspoon almond extract

*For CAUGA:*

- 2 tablespoons of water

- 1 1/2 cups pitted and chopped cherries

- ¼ teaspoon almond extract

**Indications:**

1. Put the almond milk in the slow cooker.

2. Add 2 cups of water, oatmeal, cocoa powder, 1/3 cup of cherries, maple syrup, and ½ teaspoon of almond extract.

3. Stir, cover and simmer for 8 hours.

4. In a small saucepan, mix 2 tablespoons of water with 1 ½ cups of cherries and ¼ teaspoon of almond extract, mix well, bring to a boil over medium heat and cook for 10 minutes until thick.

5. Divide oatmeal into breakfast bowls, garnish with cherry sauce, and serve.

**Nutrition:** 150 calories, 1 fat, 2 fibers, 6 carbohydrates, 5 proteins

# Crazy Maple Pear Breakfast

**Preparation Time**: 10 mins

**Cooking Time**: 9 hrs

**Servings**: 2

**Ingredients:**

- 1 pear, cored and minced
- ½ teaspoon maple extract
- 2 cups coconut milk
- ½ cup steel cut oats
- ½ teaspoon vanilla extract
- 1 tablespoon stevia
- ¼ cup of chopped walnuts to serve
- sight spray

**Indications:**

1. Spray slow cooker with cooking spray and add coconut milk.

2. Also add the maple extract, oatmeal, pear, stevia and vanilla extract, mix, cover and simmer for 9 hours.

3. Stir the oats again, divide into breakfast bowls, and serve with the chopped walnuts on top.

**Nutrition**: 150 calories, 3 fats, 2 fibers, 6 carbohydrates, 6 proteins

# Generous Bowls Of French Toast

**Preparation Time**: 10 mins

**Cooking Time**: 5 hs

**Servings**: 4

**Ingredients:**

- 1 1/2 cups of almond milk
- 1 cup of coconut cream
- 1 tablespoon vanilla extract
- ½ tablespoon ground cinnamon
- 2 tablespoons maple syrup
- 2 apples, cored and diced
- ½ cup dried cranberries
- 1 pound vegan bread
- sight spray

**Indications:**

1. Spray the slow cooker with a little cooking spray and add the bread.

2. Also, add the blueberries and apples and mix gently.

3. Add milk, coconut cream, maple syrup, vanilla extract, ground cinnamon, and spray.

4. Stir, cover and simmer for 5 hours.

5. Divide into bowls and serve immediately.

**Nutrition**: 140 calories, 2 fats, 3 fibers, 6 carbohydrates, 2 proteins

# Tofu Burrito

**Preparation Time**: 10 mins

**Cooking Time**: 8 hrs

**Servings**: 4

**Ingredients**:

- 15 ounces canned black beans, drained
- 2 tablespoons minced onion
- 7 ounces tofu, drained and crumbled
- 2 tablespoons green bell pepper, chopped
- ½ teaspoon turmeric
- cup of water
- ¼ teaspoon smoked paprika
- teaspoon cumin
- teaspoon chili powder
- a pinch of salt and black pepper
- 4 gluten-free whole wheat tortillas
- chopped avocado to serve
- sauce to serve

**Indications:**

1. Put the black beans in the slow cooker.

2. Add onion, tofu, bell pepper, turmeric, water, paprika, cumin, chili powder, a pinch of salt and pepper, mix, cover and simmer for 8 hours.

3. Divide into each tortilla, add the avocado and sauce, wrap, arrange on plates and serve

**Nutrition**: 130 calories, 4 fats, 2 fibers, 5 carbohydrates, 4 proteins

# Delicious Banana Bread

**Preparation Time**: 10 mins

**Cooking Time**: 4 hrs

**Servings**: 6

## Ingredients:

- 1 teaspoon of baking powder
- 3 bananas (mashed)
- 2 cups of whole wheat flour
- ½ teaspoon baking soda
- 1 cup palm sugar
- 2 tablespoons of flax flour + 1 tablespoon of water
- ½ cup coconut butter, melted

## Indications:

1. In a bowl, mix the sugar with the flour, baking soda and baking powder and mix.

2. Add the flax flour mixed with the water, butter and bananas, mix very well and pour the mixture into a greased round skillet suitable for your slow cooker.

3. Place the skillet in the slow cooker, cover and simmer for 4 hours.

4. Let the bread cool, cut it into slices and serve it for breakfast.

**Nutrition**: 160 calories, 3 fats, 3 fibers, 7 carbohydrates, 6 proteins

# Energy Bars For Breakfast

**Preparation Time**: 10 mins

**Cooking Time**: 4 hrs

**Servings**: 8

**Ingredients:**

- 1/2 teaspoon cinnamon
- 1 cup almond milk
- 1/3 cup quinoa
- 2 tablespoons chia seeds
- 1/3 cup apple, dried and chopped
- ½ cup raisins
- 2 tablespoons maple syrup
- 2 tablespoons almond butter, 1/3 cup almonds, melted, toasted and chopped
- 2 tablespoons of flax flour + 1 tablespoon of water
- sight spray

## Indications:

1. Grease your slow cooker with cooking spray and add parchment paper inside.

2. In a bowl, mix the melted almond butter with the maple syrup and beat very well.

3. Add the cinnamon and almond milk and mix everything.

4. Add the flax flour mixed with water and mix well again.

5. Transfer this to your slow cooker, add the quinoa, chia, apples and raisins, mix very well and press into the slow cooker.

6. Cook over low heat for 4 hours.

7. Remove quinoa leaf from slow cooker using parchment paper as handles, cool, slice and serve.

**Nutrition**: 140 calories, 3 fats, 2 fibers, 6 carbohydrates, 5 proteins

# Tasty Breakfast Sandwiches

**Preparation Time**: 10 mins

**Cooking Time:** 2 hrs

**Servings**: 6

**Ingredients:**

- 6 tablespoons almond milk, hot
- 4 tablespoons maple syrup
- ½ tablespoon coconut butter
- 1 teaspoon vanilla extract 2 and ¼ teaspoon baking powder 2 cups whole wheat flour
- sight spray

*For CAUGA:*

- ¼ cup walnuts, chopped
- 2 tablespoons almond milk
- 2 tablespoons coconut butter, melted 4 tablespoons maple syrup

For the filling:

- ½ tablespoon coconut butter, melted 3 tablespoons maple syrup
- 1 and ½ teaspoons ground cinnamon

**Indications:**

1. In a bowl mix 6 tablespoons of milk with ½ tablespoon of butter, 1 teaspoon of vanilla extract and 4 tablespoons of maple syrup, mix well and heat in the microwave for a few seconds.

2. Add the flour and baking powder, knead very well into a dough and set aside for now.

3. In a bowl, mix 2 tablespoons of almond milk with 2 tablespoons of coconut butter, 4 tablespoons of maple syrup and walnuts and mix well.

4. In another bowl, mix 1/2 tablespoon of coconut butter with 3 tablespoons of maple syrup and ground cinnamon and mix

5. Divide the dough into 12 rectangles and spread each one with the cinnamon filling.

6. Roll into 12 balls and dip each into the maple syrup and walnut sauce that you made.

7. Grease your slow cooker with cooking spray and top with the sweet muffins.

8. Simmer for 2 hours.

9. Allow sandwiches to cool completely before serving.

**Nutrition:** 200 calories, 4 fats, 3 fibers, 7 carbohydrates, 5 proteins

# Cornbread Casserole

**Preparation Time**: 10 mins

**Cooking Time**: 2 hrs 30 mins

**Servings**: 6

**Ingredients:**

- 3 garlic cloves, minced
- 1 green bell pepper,
- 1 yellow onion
- 15 ounces canned black beans, drained
- 15 ounces canned kidney beans, drained 15 ounces canned pinto beans, drained
- 15 ounces canned tomatoes, chopped 10 ounces tomato sauce
- 2 teaspoons of chili powder
- 10 ounces canned corn
- 1 teaspoon hot sauce

- a pinch of salt and pepper

- ½ cup yellow cornmeal

- ½ cup of almond flour

- 1 and 1/4 teaspoon baking powder

- 1 tablespoon palm sugar

- cup of almond milk

- 1 tablespoon chia seeds

- 1 1/2 tablespoons vegetable oil

- sight spray

**Indications:**

1. Heat a skillet over medium-high heat, add garlic, bell pepper, and onion, brown for 7 minutes, and transfer to slow cooker after dusting with cooking spray.

2. Add the black beans, borlotti beans, kidney beans, tomatoes, tomato sauce, corn, chili powder, salt, pepper and hot sauce, stir, cover and cook on full power to 1 hour.

3. Meanwhile, in a bowl, mix the almond flour with the cornmeal, baking powder, sugar, milk, chia seeds and vegetable oil and mix well.

4. Add to slow cooker and spread out.

5. Return to slow cooker and cook on full power for an additional 1 hour and 30 minutes.

6. Allow cornbread to cool before cutting and serving.

**Nutrition:** 240 calories, 4 fats, 2 fibers, 6 carbohydrates, 9 proteins

# Pumpkin Walnut Oatmeal

**Preparation Time**: 10 mins

**Cooking Time**: 8 hrs

**Servings**: 4

**Ingredients:**

- 1 1/2 cups of water
- ½ cup pumpkin puree
- 3 tablespoons of stevia
- 1 teaspoon of pumpkin pie spice
- ½ cup steel cut oats
- ¼ cup walnuts, chopped

**Indications:**

1. In slow cooker, mix water with oats, pumpkin puree, pumpkin spice, and stevia, mix, cover, and simmer for 8 hours.

2. Sprinkle with walnuts, toss, divide into bowls and serve for breakfast.

**Nutrition**: 211 calories, 4 fats, 7 fibers, 8 carbohydrates, 3 proteins

# Tasty Burrito Breakfast

**Preparation Time**: 10 mins

**Cooking Time:** 6 hours

**Servings**: 8

**Ingredients:**

- 16 ounces tofu, crumbled
- 1 green bell pepper, chopped
- ¼ cup minced shallots
- 15 ounces canned black beans, drained 1 cup vegan salsa
- ½ cup of water
- teaspoon cumin, ground
- ½ teaspoon turmeric powder
- ½ teaspoon smoked paprika
- a pinch of salt and black pepper.
- teaspoon chili powder
- 3 cups spinach leaves, 8 broken vegan tortillas to serve

**Indications:**

1. In the slow cooker, mix the tofu with bell pepper, shallot, black beans, sauce, water, cumin, turmeric, paprika, salt, pepper and chili powder, mix, cover and simmer for 6 hours.

2. Add the spinach, mix well, divide it into your vegan omelettes, roll it up, wrap it and serve it for breakfast.

**Nutrition**: 211 calories, 4 fats, 7 fibers, 14 carbohydrates, 4 proteins

# Healthy Steel Cut Oats

**Preparation Time**: 10 minutes

**Cooking Time**: 4 hrs

**Servings**: 6

**Ingredients:**

- 1 1/2 cups of water
- 1 1/2 cups coconut milk
- 1 cup steel cut oats
- 2 apples
- ½ teaspoon ground cinnamon
- ¼ teaspoon ground nutmeg
- ¼ teaspoon allspice, ground
- ¼ teaspoon ground ginger
- ¼ teaspoon ground cardamom
- 1 tablespoon flaxseed, ground
- 2 teaspoons vanilla extract
- 2 teaspoons of stevia
- sight spray

**Indications:**

1. Spray slow cooker with cooking spray, add apple chunks, milk, water, cinnamon, oatmeal, allspice, nutmeg, cardamom, ginger, vanilla, flaxseed and stevia, mix, cover and cook over heat slow for 4 hours.

2. Stir the oats again, divide into bowls, and serve.

**Nutrition**: 162 calories, 3 fats, 7 fibers, 8 carbohydrates, 5 proteins

# Tofu Casserole For Breakfast

**Preparation Time**: 10 mins

**Cooking Time**: 4 hrs

**Servings**: 4

## Ingredients:

- 1 teaspoon lemon zest, 14 ounces grated
-  tofu, diced
- 1 tablespoon of lemon juice
- 2 tablespoons nutritional yeast
- 1 tablespoon apple cider vinegar
- 1 tablespoon olive oil
- 2 garlic cloves, minced
- 10 ounces spinach, torn
- 1/2 cup yellow onion, chopped
- ½ teaspoon dried basil
- 8 ounces mushrooms, sliced
- salt and black pepper to taste
- ¼ teaspoon red chili flakes
- sight spray

## Indications:

1. Sprinkle some cooking spray into the slow cooker and place the tofu cubes on the bottom.

2. Add the lemon zest, lemon juice, baking powder, vinegar, olive oil, garlic, spinach, onion, basil, mushrooms, salt, pepper and pepper flakes, mix, cover and simmer for 4 hours.

3. Divide into plates and serve for breakfast.

**Nutrition:** 216 calories, 6 fats, 8 fibers, 12 carbohydrates, 4 proteins

# Vegan Vegetarian Sauce

**Preparation Time:** 10 mins

**Cooking Time**: 7 hrs

**Servings**: 4

**Ingredients**:

- 1 cup carrots, sliced
- 1/3 cup cashews
- 1 1/2 cups of cauliflower florets
- ½ cup chopped turnips
- 2 ½ cups water
- 1 cup of almond milk
- 1 teaspoon garlic powder
- cup nutritional yeast
- ¼ teaspoon smoked paprika
- ¼ teaspoon mustard powder
- pinch of salt

**Indications:**

1. In your slow cooker, toss carrots with cauliflower, cashews, turnips and water, toss, cover and simmer for 7 hours.

2. Drain, transfer to a blender, add the almond milk, garlic powder, baking powder, paprika, mustard powder and salt, mix well and serve as a snack.

**Nutrition**: 291 calories, 7 fats, 4 fibers, 14 carbohydrates, 3 proteins

# Great Bolognese Sauce

**Preparation Time**: 10 mins

**Cooking Time**: 5 hrs

**Servings**: 7

**Ingredients:**

- ½ head of cauliflower, mashed
- 54 ounces canned tomatoes, mashed
- 10 ounces white mushrooms, chopped
- 2 cups carrots, grated
- 2 cups aubergine, diced
- 6 garlic cloves, minced
- 2 tablespoons agave nectar
- 2 tablespoons tomato paste
- 2 tablespoons balsamic vinegar
- 1 tablespoon basil, chopped
- 1 1/2 tablespoons minced oregano
- 1 1/2 teaspoons dried rosemary
- a pinch of salt and black pepper

**Indications:**

1. In the slow cooker, mix the cauliflower rice with tomatoes, mushrooms, carrots, diced aubergine, garlic, agave nectar, balsamic vinegar, tomato paste, rosemary, salt and pepper, mix, cover and cook until high heat for 5 hours.

2. Add the basil and oregano, mix again, divide into bowls and serve as a sauce.

**Nutrition**: 251 calories, 7 fats, 6 fibers, 10 carbohydrates, 6 proteins

# Black-Eyed Pea Pate

**Preparation Time**: 10 mins

**Cooking Time**: 5 hrs

**Servings:** 5

## Ingredients:

- 1 ½ cups of peas with the eye
- 3 cups of water
- 1 teaspoon of ajun seasoning
- ½ cup of toasted walnuts
- ½ teaspoon garlic powder
- ½ teaspoon jalapeño powder
- a pinch of salt and black pepper.
- ¼ teaspoon liquid smoke
- ½ teaspoon Tabasco sauce

## Indications:

1. In the slow cooker, mix the black-eyed beans with the ajun seasoning, salt, pepper and water, stir, cover and cook over high heat for 5 hours.

2. Drain, transfer to a blender, add walnuts, garlic powder, jalapeño powder, Tabasco sauce, liquid smoke, more salt and pepper, blend well and serve as an appetizer.

**Nutrition**: 221 calories, 4 fats, 7 fibers, 16 carbohydrates, 4 proteins

# Hearty Breakfast Casserole

**Preparation Time**: 10 mins

**Cooking Time:** 4 hrs

**Servings:** 4

**Ingredients:**

- 2 teaspoons of onion powder
- ¾ cup of cashews, soaked for about 30 mins and well drained
- 1 teaspoon of garlic powder
- ¼ cup of nutritional yeast
- ½ teaspoon of dried sage
- black pepper and salt
- 1 yellow onion, chopped
- 3 garlic cloves
- 2 tablespoons parsley,
- 4 red potatoes, cubed
- 1 tablespoon olive oil
- ½ teaspoon of red pepper flakes

**Indications:**

1. Mix cashews with onion powder, nutritional yeast, garlic powder, sage, salt and pepper in your blender and pulse really well.

2. Add some oil to your slow cooker.

3. Add potatoes, garlic, onion, pepper flakes, salt, parsley and pepper

4. Add some cashews sauce, cover and cook on high heat for about 4 hours.

5. Serve on plates for breakfast.

**Nutrition**: 218 calories, fat 6, 6 fiber, 14 carbohydrates, 5 protein

# Carrot and Coconut Soup

**Preparation Time**: 10 mins

**Cooking Time**: 7 hrs

**Servings:** 6

**Ingredients:**

- 1 sweet potato, diced
- 2 pounds baby carrots, peeled
- 2 teaspoons ginger paste
- 1 yellow onion, minced
- 4 cups vegetable broth
- 2 teaspoons curry powder
- salt and black pepper to taste
- 14 ounces coconut milk

**Indications:**

1. In slow cooker, combine sweet potato with carrots, ginger paste, onion, broth, curry powder, salt and pepper, stir, cover and cook on full power for 7 hours.

2. Add the coconut milk, blend the soup with a hand mixer, divide the soup into bowls and serve.

**Nutrition**: 100 calories, 2 fats, 4 fibers, 18 carbohydrates, 3 proteins

# Chinese Carrot Cream

**Preparation Time**: 10 mins

**Cooking Time:** 5 hrs

**Servings:** 6

## Ingredients:

- 1 tablespoon coconut oil
- 3 garlic cloves, minced
- 1 yellow onion, minced
- 1 pound carrots, chopped
- 2 cups vegetable broth
- 2 cups of water
- salt and black pepper to taste
- 1/3 cup peanut butter
- 2 teaspoons chili sauce

## Indications:

1. In the slow cooker, mix the oil with the garlic, onion, carrots, broth, water, salt, pepper and chili sauce, mix, cover and cook over high heat for 4 hours and 30 minutes.

2. Add the peanut butter, mix, cover, cook the soup for another 30 minutes, mix with a hand mixer, divide the soup into bowls and serve.

**Nutrition**: 224 calories, 14 fats, 6 fibers, 18 carbohydrates, 7 proteins

# Seitan Stew

**Preparation Time**: 10 mins

**Cooking Time**: 7 hrs

**Servings:** 4

**Ingredients:**

- 1 pound seitan, minced
- 2 tablespoons coconut aminos
- 1 yellow onion, chopped
- 5 cups vegetable broth
- 2 chopped tomatoes
- 3 garlic cloves, minced
- 3 potatoes, cubed
- 3 carrots, chopped
- 2 celery stalks, chopped
- salt and black pepper to taste

**Indications:**

1. In your slow cooker, mix the seitan with the amino acids, onion, broth, tomatoes, garlic, potatoes, carrots, celery, salt and pepper, mix, cover and cook over heat. slow for 7 hours.

2. Divide into bowls and serve.

**Nutrition**: 300 calories, 4 fats, 6 fibers, 12 carbohydrates, 3 proteins

# Spicy Carrot Stew

**Preparation Time**: 10 mins

**Cooking Time**: 3 hrs

**Servings**: 6

**Ingredients:**

- 1 pound carrots, peeled and sliced with a spiralizer
- 1 cup red onion, minced
- 2 garlic cloves, minced
- 2 celery sticks, minced
- 1 teaspoon of ground cumin
- 1 teaspoon ground coriander
- ½ teaspoon ground turmeric
- pinch ground cinnamon
- 1 cup of water
- salt and black pepper to taste
- 4 cups of vegetable broth
- 1 cup of lentils
- 15 ounces canned tomatoes, chopped
- 1 tablespoon tomato paste
- ¼ cup cilantro, chopped
- 1 tablespoon of lemon juice
- 1 tablespoon hot pepper sauce

**Indications:**

1. In the slow cooker, combine the carrots with the onion, garlic, celery, coriander, cumin, turmeric, cinnamon, salt, pepper, water, broth, lentils, tomatoes, tomato paste and pepper sauce, mix, cover and cook for 3 hours.

2. Add the lemon juice and cilantro, mix, divide into bowls and serve.

**Nutrition**: 218 calories, 4 fats, 4 fibers, 8 carbohydrates, 3 proteins

# Tomato Soup

**Preparation Time**: 10 mins

**Cooking Time**: 4 hrs

**Servings**: 6

## Ingredients:

- 2 pounds and diced tomatoes
- 3 ½ cups vegetable broth
- 1 yellow onion, chopped
- 2 tablespoons tomato paste
- 2 teaspoons dried basil
- ½ teaspoon cumin, ground
- salt and black pepper to taste
- 2/3 cup almond milk

## Indications:

1. In the slow cooker, mix the tomatoes with the vegetable broth, onion, tomato paste, basil, cumin, salt and pepper, mix, cover and simmer for 4 hours.

2. Add the almond milk, blend the soup with a hand mixer, pour into bowls and serve.

**Nutrition**: 212 calories, 4 fats, 4 fibers, 8 carbohydrates, 5 proteins

# Classic Tomato Soup

**Preparation Time**: 10 mins

**Cooking Time:** 8 hrs

**Servings**: 4

## Ingredients:

- 1 tablespoon of olive oil
- 1 teaspoon minced garlic
- 1 red bell pepper, minced
- 1 yellow onion, minced
- 45 ounces canned tomatoes, chopped
- 1 cup vegetable broth
- salt and black pepper to taste
- a pinch of red pepper flakes
- 1 tablespoon basil, chopped

## Indications:

1. In the slow cooker, mix the oil with the onion, bell pepper, garlic, tomatoes, broth, salt and pepper, mix, cover and simmer for 8 hours.

2. Blend with an immersion blender, add the bell pepper flakes and basil, mix, pour into bowls and serve.

**Nutrition**: 100 calories, 2 fat, 4 fibers, 8 carbohydrates, 4 proteins

# Vegan Chickpea Winter Mix

**Preparation Time**: 10 mins

**Cooking Time**: 4 hrs 10 mins

**Servings**: 6

**Ingredients:**

- 1 yellow onion, chopped
- 1 tablespoon grated ginger
- 1 tablespoon olive oil
- 4 garlic cloves, minced
- pinch of salt and black pepper
- 2 Thai red chili peppers, chopped
- ½ teaspoon turmeric powder
- 2 tablespoons garam masala
- 4 ounces tomato paste
- 2 cups of vegetable broth
- 6 ounces canned chickpeas, drained
- 2 tablespoons chopped cilantro

**Indications:**

1. Heat a skillet with oil over medium-high heat, add the ginger and onion, mix and cook for 4-5 minutes.

2. Add garlic, salt, pepper, Thai chilies, garam masala, and turmeric, stir, cook for another 2 minutes, and transfer to slow cooker.

3. Add the broth, chickpeas and tomato paste, mix, cover and cook over low heat for 4 hours.

4. Add the cilantro, toss, divide into bowls and serve.

5. Enjoy!

**Nutrition:** 211 calories, 7 fats, 4 fibers, 9 carbohydrates, 7 proteins

# Indian Lentil Mix

**Preparation Time**: 10 mins

**Cooking Time**: 8 hrs

**Servings**: 16

**Ingredients:**

- 4 garlic cloves, minced
- 4 cups brown lentils
- 2 yellow onions, minced
- 1 tablespoon grated ginger
- 4 tablespoons olive oil
- 1 tablespoon garam masala
- 4 tablespoons red curry paste
- 2 teaspoons stevia
- 1 ½ teaspoon turmeric powder
- pinch of salt and black pepper
- 45 ounces canned tomato puree
- ½ cup coconut milk
- 1 tablespoon coriander chopped

**Indications:**

1. In the slow cooker, mix the lentils with onion, garlic, ginger, oil, curry paste, garam masala, turmeric, salt, pepper, and stevia.

2. Also add the tomato puree, mix, cover and simmer for 7 hours and 20 minutes.

3. Add the coconut milk and cilantro, mix, cover and simmer for 40 minutes.

4. Divide into bowls and serve.

5. Enjoy!

**Nutrition**: 118 calories, 5 fats, 4 fibers, 18 carbohydrates, 4 proteins

# Bean Stew

**Preparation Time**: 10 mins

**Cooking Time**: 12 hrs

**Servings**: 6

## Ingredients:

- 1 pound marinated kidney beans, soaked overnight and drained
- 1 cup maple syrup
- 1 cup vegan barbecue sauce
- 4 tablespoons stevia
- 1 cup of water
- ¼ cup tomato paste
- mustard cup
- cup olive oil
- cup apple cider vinegar
- 2 tablespoons coconut amino acids

## Indications:

1. In the slow cooker, mix the beans with the maple syrup, barbecue sauce, stevia, water, tomato paste, mustard, oil, vinegar and amino acids, mix, cover and simmer for 12 hours.

2. Divide into bowls and serve hot.

**Nutrition**: 453 calories, 7 fats, 12 fibers, 40 carbohydrates, 13 proteins

# Pumpkin Chili

**Preparation Time**: 10 mins

**Cooking Time**: 6 hrs

**Servings**: 8

**Ingredients:**

- 2 carrots, chopped
- 1 yellow onion, minced
- 2 stalks of celery, minced
- 2 green apples, cored, peeled and minced
- 4 garlic cloves, minced
- 2 cups butternut squash, peeled and diced
- 180g canned chickpeas, drained
- 6 ounces canned black beans, drained
- 7 ounces canned coconut milk
- 2 teaspoons chili powder
- 1 teaspoon dried oregano
- 1 tablespoon ground cumin
- 2 cups vegetable broth
- 2 tablespoons tomato paste
- salt and black pepper to taste
- 1 tablespoon chopped coriander

**Indications:**

1. In slow cooker, mix carrots with onion, celery, apples, garlic, squash, chickpeas, black beans, coconut milk, chili powder, oregano, cumin, broth, tomato paste, salt and pepper, mix, cover and cook on High for 6 hours.

2. Add the cilantro, toss, divide into bowls and serve.

**Nutrition:** 312 calories, 6 fats, 8 fibers, 12 carbohydrates, 6 proteins

# Rich Lentil Soup

**Preparation Time:** 10 mins

**Cooking Time**: 2 hrs 30 mins

**Servings**: 4

**Ingredients:**

- 2 teaspoons minced garlic
- 1 tablespoon olive oil
- 1 yellow onion
- 1 teaspoon cumin
- 1 teaspoon coriander seeds
- 1 teaspoon turmeric powder
- 1 teaspoon ground cinnamon
- ½ teaspoon garam masala
- 1 ½ cup red lentils
- 4 cups of vegetable broth
- 14 oz. coconut milk
- 4 cups spinach
- salt and black pepper to taste

**Indications:**

1. In the slow cooker, mix the garlic, oil, onion, cumin, coriander, turmeric, cinnamon, garam masala, lentils, and broth, stir, cover, and cook on full power for 2 hours.

2. Add the coconut, spinach, salt and pepper, mix and cook over high heat for another 30 minutes.

3. Pour into bowls and serve.

**Nutrition**: 271 calories, 6 fats, 5 fibers, 8 carbohydrates, 4 proteins

# Rhubarb Stew

**Preparation Time**: 10 mins

**Cooking Time**: 7 hrs

**Servings**: 4

**Ingredients:**

- 5 cups of rhubarb
- 2 tablespoons coconut butter
- 1/3 cup water
- 2/3 cup coconut sugar
- 1 teaspoon vanilla extract

**Indications**:

1. Put the rhubarb in the slow cooker.

2. Add the water and sugar, mix gently, cover and simmer for 7 hours.

3. Add the coconut butter and vanilla extract, mix and refrigerate until chilled.

**Nutrition**: 120 calories, 2 fats, 3 fibers, 6 carbohydrates, 1 protein

# Pudding Cake

**Preparation Time:** 10 mins

**Cooking Time**: 2 hrs 30 mins

**Servings**: 8

**Ingredients:**

- 1 1/2 cups of stevia
- 1 cup of flour
- ¼ cup baking cocoa + 2 tablespoons
- ½ cup almond milk chocolate
- 2 teaspoons baking powder
- 2 tablespoons canola oil
- 1 teaspoon vanilla extract
- 1 1/2 cups hot water
- sight spray

**Indications:**

1. In a bowl mix the flour with 2 tablespoons of cocoa, baking powder, almond milk, oil and vanilla extract, mix well and spread on the bottom of the slow cooker after greasing it with cooking spray.

2. In a separate bowl, mix the stevia with the rest of the cocoa and water, mix well, and spread over the batter in the slow cooker.

3. Finally, bake your cake on high for 2 hours and 30 minutes.

4. Let the cake cool, cut into slices and serve.

**Nutrition:** 250 calories, 4 fats, 3 fibers, 40 carbohydrates, 2 proteins

# Sweet Peanut Butter Cake

**Preparation Time**: 10 mins

**Cooking Time:** 2 hrs 30 mins

**Servings**: 8

## Ingredients:

- 1 cup coconut sugar
- 1 cup flour
- 3 tablespoons cocoa powder + ½ cup
- 1 and ½ teaspoons baking powder
- ½ cup of almond milk
- 2 tablespoons coconut oil
- 2 cups hot water
- 1 teaspoon vanilla extract
- ½ cup peanut butter
- sight spray

## Indications:

1. In a bowl, mix half of the coconut sugar with 3 tablespoons of cocoa, flour and yeast and mix well.

2. Add coconut oil, vanilla and milk, mix well and pour into slow cooker greased with cooking spray.

3. In another bowl, mix remaining sugar with remaining cocoa, peanut butter, and hot water, mix well, and pour over batter in slow cooker.

4. On the pot, cook on full power for 2 hours and 30 minutes, cut the cake and serve.

**Nutrition**: 242 calories, 4 fats, 7 fibers, 8 carbohydrates, 4 proteins

# Cranberry Cake

**Preparation Time**: 10 mins

**Cooking Time**: 1 hr

**Servings**: 6

**Ingredients:**

- ½ cup whole wheat flour
- ¼ teaspoon baking powder
- teaspoon stevia
- ¼ cup blueberries
- 1/3 cup almond milk
- 1 teaspoon flax seeds
- ½ teaspoon grated lemon zest
- ¼ teaspoon vanilla extract
- ¼ teaspoon lemon extract
- sight spray

**Indications:**

1. In a bowl, mix the flour with the baking powder and stevia and mix.

2. Add the blueberries, milk, oil, flax seeds, lemon zest, vanilla extract, and lemon extract and mix well.

3. Spray your slow cooker with cooking spray, cover with parchment paper, pour in cake batter, cover pot and cook over high heat for 1 hour.

4. Let the cake cool, cut into slices and serve.

**Nutrition:** 200 calories, 4 fats, 4 fibers, 10 carbohydrates, 4 proteins

# Peach Pie

**Preparation Time**: 10 mins

**Cooking Time**: 4 hrs

**Servings:** 4

**Ingredients:**

- 4 cups peaches, peeled and sliced
- cup coconut sugar
- ½ teaspoon ground cinnamon
- 1 1/2 cups vegan sweet cookies, crushed
- cup of stevia
- ¼ teaspoon ground nutmeg
- ½ cup of almond milk
- 1 teaspoon vanilla extract
- sight spray

**Indications:**

1. In a bowl, mix the peaches with the coconut sugar and cinnamon and mix.

2. In a separate bowl, mix the cookies with the stevia, nutmeg, almond milk, and vanilla extract and mix.

3. Spray slow cooker with cooking spray and sprinkle peaches on bottom.

4. Add cookie mix, spread, cover and simmer 4 hours.

5. Divide shoe rack among plates and serve.

6. Enjoy!

**Nutrition**: 212 calories, 4 fats, 4 fibers, 7 carbohydrates, 3 proteins

# Crazy Cauliflower Zucchini Surprise

**Preparation Time**: 10 minutes

**Cooking Time**: 3 hours 30 minutes

**Servings**: 4

## Ingredients:

- 1 head of cauliflower, sprigs separated
- 2 garlic cloves, minced
- ¾ cup red onion, minced
- 1 teaspoon dried basil
- 2 teaspoons oregano flakes
- 28 ounces canned tomatoes, chopped
- ¼ teaspoon red chili flakes
- ½ cup vegetable broth
- 5 spiralized zucchini
- pinch of salt
- black pepper to taste

## Indications:

1. Place cauliflower florets in slow cooker.

2. Add garlic, onion, basil, oregano, tomatoes, broth, red pepper flakes, salt and pepper, mix, cover and cook over high heat for 3 hours and 30 minutes.

3. Mash the cauliflower a little with a potato masher.

4. Divide zucchini noodles into bowls, top each with cauliflower mixture, and serve.

**Nutrition:** 150 calories, 2 fats, 3 fibers, 6 carbohydrates, 9 proteins

# Quinoa and Vegetables

**Preparation Time**: 10 mins

**Cooking Time**: 4 hrs

**Servings**: 4

## Ingredients:

- 1 tablespoon olive oil
- 1 ½ cups quinoa
- 3 cups vegetable broth
- 1 yellow onion, chopped
- 1 carrot, chopped
- 1 sweet red bell pepper, minced
- 1 cup green beans, minced
- 2 garlic cloves, minced
- 1 teaspoon chopped coriander
- a pinch of salt
- black pepper to taste

## Indications:

1. Put the broth in the slow cooker.

2. Add oil, quinoa, onion, carrot, sweet pepper, beans, cloves, salt and pepper, mix, cover and simmer for 4 hours.

3. Add the cilantro, mix again, divide into plates and serve.

**Nutrition**: 120 calories, 2 fats, 3 fibers, 6 carbohydrates, 6 protein

# Spaghetti Bowls With Pumpkin

**Preparation Time**: 10 mims

**Cooking Time**: 8 hrs

**Servings**: 4

**Ingredients:**

- 5 pounds spaghetti squash, peeled
- 2 cups water
- 2 cups broccoli florets, steamed
- 1 tablespoon sesame seeds
- ½ peanuts with hops for serving
- ½ batch of salad dressing

*For the salad dressing:*

- 1 tablespoon of palm sugar
- 1 tablespoon of grated ginger
- 3 tablespoons of rice vinegar
- 3 tablespoons of olive oil
- 2 tablespoons peanut butter
- 1 tablespoon soy sauce
- 3 garlic cloves, minced
- 1 teaspoon sesame oil
- ½ teaspoon sesame

**Indications:**

1. In your blender, mix the ginger with sugar, vinegar, oil, soy sauce, garlic, peanut butter, sesame oil and ½ teaspoon of sesame seeds, blend very well and reserve.

2. Place the squash in the slow cooker, add the water, cover and simmer for 8 hours.

3. Allow squash to cool, cut in half, scrape off pulp and transfer to bowl.

4. Add broccoli florets, 1 tablespoon sesame seeds, chopped peanuts, and salad dressing.

5. Stir salad well and serve.

**Nutrition:** 150 calories, 4 fats, 7 fibers, 17 carbohydrates, 7 proteins

# Strawberry Jam

**Preparation Time**: 10 mins

**Cooking Time**: 4 hrs

**Servings**: 10

## Ingredients:

- 32 ounces strawberries, chopped
- 2 pounds coconut sugar
- zest of 1 lemon, 4 ounces raisins, grated
- 3 ounces of water

**Indications:**

1. In your slow cooker, mix the strawberries with the coconut sugar, lemon zest, raisins and water, mix, cover and cook over high heat for 4 hours.

2. Divide into jars and serve cold.

**Nutrition:** 100 calories, 3 fats, 2 fibers, 2 carbohydrates, 1 protein

# Lemon Marmalade

**Preparation Time**: 10 mins

**Cooking Time**: 3 hrs

**Servings:** 10

**Ingredients:**

- 2 pounds lemons, washed, peeled and sliced

- 2 pounds coconut sugar

- 1 tablespoon of vinegar

**Indications:**

1. In your slow cooker, mix the lemons with the coconut sugar and vinegar, mix, cover and cook on full power for 3 hours.

2. Divide into jars and serve cold.


**Nutrition**: 100 calories, 0 fat, 2 fibers, 7 carbohydrates, 4 proteins

# Strawberry and Rhubarb Jam

**Preparation Time**: 10 mins

**Cooking Time**: 3 hours

**Servings**: 8

**Ingredients**:

- 1/3 cup of water
- 2 pounds rhubarb, chopped
- 2 pounds strawberries, chopped
- 1 cup coconut sugar
- 1 tablespoon minced mint

## Indications:

1. In the slow cooker, mix the water with the rhubarb, strawberries, sugar and mint, mix, cover and cook over high heat for 3 hours.

2. Divide into cups and serve cold.

**Nutrition**: 100 calories, 1 fat, 4 fibers, 10 carbohydrates, 2 proteins

# Sweet Potato Pudding

**Preparation Time:** 10 mins

**Cooking time:** 5 hrs

**Servings:** 8

**Ingredients:**

- 1 cup of water
- 1 tablespoon grated lemon zest
- ½ cup coconut sugar
- 3 sweet potatoes, peeled and sliced
- ¼ cup cashew butter
- cup maple syrup
- 1 cup walnuts, chopped

**Indications:**

1. In the slow cooker, mix the water with the lemon zest, coconut sugar, potatoes, cashew butter, maple syrup and walnuts, stir, cover and cook over high heat for 5 hours.

2. Divide the sweet potato pudding into bowls and serve chilled.

**Nutrition:** 200 calories, 4 fats, 3 fibers, 10 carbohydrates, 4 proteins

# Cherry Jam

**Preparation Time**: 10 mins

**Cooking Time:** 3 hours

**Servings:** 6

**Ingredients:**

- 2 tablespoons lemon juice
- 3 tablespoons vegan gelatin
- 4 cups pitted cherries
- 2 cups of coconut sugar

**Indications:**

1. In your slow cooker, mix the lemon juice with the gelatin, cherries and coconut sugar, mix, cover and cook over high heat for 3 hours.

2. Divide into cups and serve cold.

**Nutrition:** 211 calories, 3 fats, 1 fiber, 3 carbohydrates, 3 proteins

# Rice Pudding

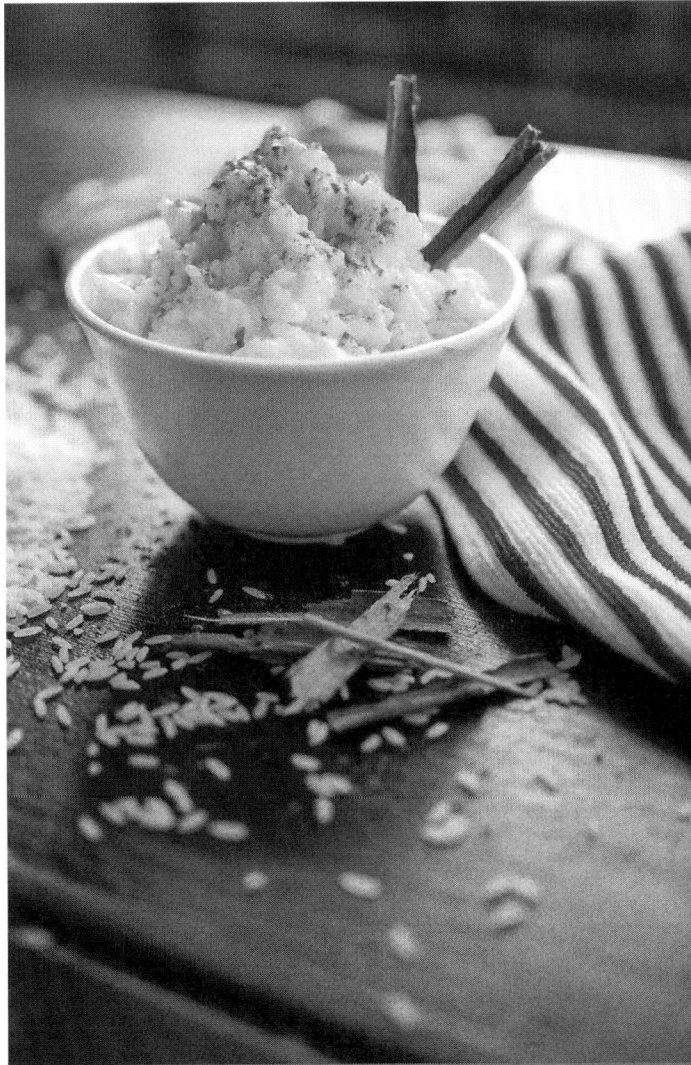

**Preparation Time:** 10 mins

**Cooking Time**: 5 hrs

**Servings:** 4

**Ingredients:**

- 6 1/2 cups of water
- 1 cup of coconut sugar
- 2 cups white rice, washed and rinsed
- 2 cinnamon sticks
- ½ cup of chopped coconut

**Indications:**

1. In your slow cooker, mix the water with the coconut sugar, rice, cinnamon and coconut, mix, cover and cook on high for 5 hours.

2. Divide the pudding into cups and serve cold.

3. Enjoy!

**Nutrition**: 213 calories, 4 fats, 6 fibers, 9 carbohydrates, 4 proteins

# Eggplant Appetizer

**Preparation Time**: 10 mins

**Cooking Time**: 7 hrs

**Servings**: 4

## Ingredients:

- 1 1/2 cups diced tomatoes
- 3 cups diced aubergine
- 2 teaspoons capers
- 180 g green olives
- 4 garlic cloves, (minced)
- 2 teaspoons balsamic vinegar
- 1 tablespoon basil, minced
- salt and black pepper to taste

## Indications:

1. In the slow cooker, mix the tomatoes with the diced aubergine, capers, green olives, garlic, vinegar, basil, salt and pepper, mix, cover and cook over low heat for 7 hours.

2. Divide into small appetizer plates and serve as an appetizer.

**Nutrition:** 200 calories, 6 fats, 5 fibers, 9 carbohydrates, 2 proteins

# Pumpkin and Spinach Mix

**Preparation Time:** 10 mins

**Cooking Time**: 3 hrs 30 mins

**Servings**: 12

**Ingredients:**

- 10 ounces spinach, chopped
- 2 pounds pumpkin, peeled and diced
- 1 cup barley
- 1 yellow onion, minced
- 14 ounces vegetable broth
- ½ cup of water
- a pinch of salt and black pepper to taste
- 3 garlic cloves, minced

**Indications:**

1. In the slow cooker, mix the pumpkin with the spinach, barley, onion, broth, water, salt, pepper and garlic, mix, cover and cook at maximum power for 3 hours and 30 minutes.

2. Divide the pumpkin mixture among plates and serve as a garnish.

**Nutrition:** 196 calories, 3 fats, 7 fibers, 36 carbohydrates, 7 proteins

# Cherry Marmalade

**Preparation Time**: 10 mins

**Cooking Time**: 3 hrs

**Servings:** 6

**Ingredients:**

- 2 tablespoons of lemon juice
- 4 cups cherries
- 3 tablespoons of vegan gelatin
- 2 cups of coconut sugar

## Indications:

1. Mix some quantity of lemon juice with gelatin, coconut sugar and cherries (in the slow cooker), stir for a while, cover and cook for 3 hours.

2. Divide into cups and you can serve cold.

**Nutrition:** fat 3, calories 211, fiber 1, protein 3, carbs 3

# Wonderful Wild Rice

**Preparation Time**: 10 mins

**Cooking Time**: 6 hrs

**Servings:** 12

**Ingredients:**

- 42 ounces vegetable broth
- 1 cup carrot, chopped
- 2 ½ cups wild rice
- 4 ounces mushrooms, sliced
- 2 tablespoons olive oil
- 2 teaspoons dried marjoram
- a pinch of sea salt
- black pepper to taste
- 2/3 cups cherries, dried
- ½ cup of chopped walnuts
- 2/3 cup green onions, chopped

**Indications:**

1. Put the broth in the slow cooker.

2. Add the rice, carrot, mushrooms, oil, salt, pepper, and marjoram.

3. Stir, cover and simmer for 6 hours.

4. Add cherries and chives, toss, cover slow cooker, and steep 10 minutes.

5. Divide the wild rice into plates and serve with the chopped walnuts on top.

**Nutrition:** 140 calories, 2 fats, 3 fibers, 6 carbohydrates, 7 protein

# Tofu Appetizer

**Preparation Time**: 10 mins

**Cooking Time**: 7 hrs

**Servings**: 6

**Ingredients:**

- ¼ cup sliced yellow onions
- 14 ounces hard tofu
- 1 cup sliced carrot

*For CAUGA:*

- ¼ cup soy sauce
- ½ cup of water
- 3 tablespoons agave nectar
- 3 tablespoons nutritional yeast
- 1 teaspoon minced garlic
- 1 tablespoon minced ginger
- ½ tablespoon of rice vinegar

## Indications:

1. In the slow cooker, mix the tofu with the onion and carrots.

2. In a bowl, mix the soy sauce with water, agave nectar, yeast, garlic, ginger and vinegar and mix well.

3. Add to slow cooker, cover and simmer 7 hours.

4. Divide into appetizer bowls and serve.

**Nutrition**: 251 calories, 6 fats, 8 fibers, 12 carbohydrates, 3 proteins

# Wonderful Blueberry Butter

**Preparation Time**: 10 mins

**Cooking Time**: 6 hrs

**Servings:** 12

**Ingredients:**

- 5 cups cranberry puree
- 2 teaspoons ground cinnamon
- The zest of 1 lemon
- 1 cup coconut sugar
- ½ teaspoon ground nutmeg
- ¼ teaspoon ground ginger

**Indications:**

1. Place the blueberries in the slow cooker, cover and simmer for 1 hour.

2. Add the berry puree, cover and simmer for another 4 hours.

3. Add the sugar, ginger, nutmeg and lemon zest, mix and cook on high heat without a lid for an additional hour.

4. Divide into jars, cover and store in a cool place until serving for breakfast.

**Nutrition:** 143 calories, 2 fats, 3 fibers, 3 carbohydrates, 4 proteins

# Delicious Pumpkin Butter

**Preparation Time**: 10 mins

**Cooking Time**: 4 hrs

**Servings**: 5

**Ingredients:**

- 2 teaspoons ground cinnamon
- 4 cups pumpkin puree
- 1 ¼ cups maple syrup
- ½ teaspoon of nutmeg
- 1 teaspoon vanilla extract

**Indications:**

1. In the slow cooker, mix the pumpkin puree with the maple syrup and vanilla extract, mix, cover and cook over high heat for 4 hours.

2. Add the cinnamon and nutmeg, mix, divide into jars and serve for breakfast.

**Nutrition**: 120 calories, 2 fats, 2 fibers, 4 carbohydrates, 2 proteins

# Delicious Quinoa Breakfast

**Preparation Time**: 10 mins

**Cooking Time**: 8 hrs

**Servings:** 4

**Ingredients:**

- 2 cups of water
- 1 cup of coconut milk
- 2 tablespoons maple syrup
- 1 cup quinoa, rinsed
- 1 teaspoon vanilla extract
- berries to serve

**Indications:**

1. Put the water in the slow cooker.

2. Add milk, maple syrup and quinoa, mix, cover and simmer for 8 hours.

3. Peel the quinoa, mix a little, divide into bowls, add the vanilla extract, mix and serve with your favorite berries on top.

**Nutrition**: 120 calories, 2 fat, 1 fiber, 4 carbohydrates, 4 protein

# Apple Crumb

**Preparation Time:** 10 mins

**Cooking Time:** 4 hrs

**Servings:** 4

**Ingredients:**

- 1 cup granola
- 2 apples, peeled, cored and chopped
- 1/8 cup maple syrup
- 2 tablespoons coconut butter
- cup apple juice
- 1/2 teaspoon ground nutmeg
- 1 teaspoon ground cinnamon

143

**Indications:**

1. Place apples in slow cooker.

2. Add the maple syrup, butter, apple juice, nutmeg, and cinnamon.

3. Stir gently, sprinkle with granola, cover, and simmer 4 hours.

4. Divide into bowls and serve.

**Nutrition:** 160 calories, 1 fat, 2 fibers, 4 carbohydrates, 5 proteins

# Delicious Banana and Coconut Milk Delight

**Preparation Time**: 10 mins

**Cooking Time**: 7 hrs

**Servings**: 6

**Ingredients:**

- 2 cups bananas, peeled and sliced
- 28 ounces canned coconut milk
- 1 cup steel cut oats
- ½ cup of water
- 2 tablespoons palm sugar
- 1 1/2 tablespoons coconut butter
- ¼ teaspoon ground nutmeg
- ½ teaspoon ground cinnamon
- 1 tablespoon flax seeds, ground
- ½ teaspoon vanilla extract
- pinch of sea salt
- chopped walnuts for serving
- sight spray

**Indications:**

1. Grease your slow cooker with cooking spray and add coconut milk.

2. Also add bananas, oatmeal, water, palm sugar, coconut butter, cinnamon, nutmeg, flax seeds, and a pinch of salt.

3. Stir, cover and simmer for 7 hours.

4. Divide into bowls and serve with chopped walnuts on top.

**Nutrition**: 150 calories, 2 fats, 1 fiber, 5 carbohydrates, 7 proteins

# Flavored Beetroot

**Preparation Time**: 10 mins

**Cooking Time**: 8 hrs

**Servings:** 6

## Ingredients:

- 6 beets, peeled and cut into wedges
- pinch of sea salt
- black pepper to taste
- 2 tablespoons olive oil
- 2 tablespoons lemon juice
- 1 tablespoon cider vinegar
- 2 tablespoons agave nectar
- ½ teaspoon lemon zest, grated
- 2 sprigs rosemary

## Indications:

1. Place beets in slow cooker.

2. Add a pinch of salt, black pepper, lemon juice, oil, agave nectar, rosemary, and vinegar.

3. Mix everything, cover and cook over low heat for 8 hours.

4. Add the lemon zest, mix, divide into plates and serve.

**Nutrition:** 120 calories, 1 fat, 2 fiber, 6 carbohydrates, 6 protein

# Excellent Dish Of Beans and Lentils

**Preparation Time**: 10 mins

**Cooking Time**: 7 hrs 10 mins

**Servings:** 6

**Ingredients:**

- 2 tablespoons minced thyme
- 5 cups of water
- 1 tablespoon olive oil
- 1 cup of chopped yellow onion
- 5 garlic cloves
- 3 tablespoons apple cider vinegar
- ½ cup tomato paste
- ½ cup maple syrup
- 3 tablespoons soy sauce
- 2 tablespoons dry mustard
- 2 tablespoons Korean red pepper paste
- 1 1/2 cups large northern beans
- ½ cup red lentils

**Indications:**

1. Heat a skillet with the oil over medium-high heat, add the onion, stir and cook for 4 minutes.

2. Add the garlic, thyme, vinegar, and tomato paste, stir, cook for another 5 minutes, and transfer to the slow cooker.

3. Add the lentils and beans to the slow cooker and mix.

4. Also add the water, maple syrup, mustard, chili paste, and soy sauce, mix, cover, and cook on full power for 7 hours.

5. Stir beans again, divide into plates, and serve.

**Nutrition**: 160 calories, 2 fats, 4 fibers, 7 carbohydrates, 8 proteins

# Easy Sweet Potato Dish

**Preparation Time:** 10 mins

**Cooking Time:** 6 hrs

**Servings**: 6

**Ingredients:**

- 4 pounds sweet potatoes, peeled and sliced
- ½ cup of orange juice
- 3 tablespoons palm sugar
- ½ teaspoon dried thyme
- a pinch of sea salt
- black pepper to taste
- ½ teaspoon dried sage
- 2 tablespoons olive oil

**Indications:**

1. Put the oil in the slow cooker and add the sweet potato slices.

2. In a bowl, mix the orange juice with the palm sugar, thyme, sage, a pinch of salt and black pepper and mix well.

3. Add to potatoes, stir to coat, cover slow cooker, and simmer 6 hours.

4. Stir the sweet potatoes again, divide into plates and serve.

**Nutrition**: 160 calories, 3 fats, 2 fibers, 6 carbohydrates, 9 proteins

*Finally, if you've found this book helpful in any way,*
*an Amazon review is always welcome!*

Printed in Great Britain
by Amazon